Independence Matters

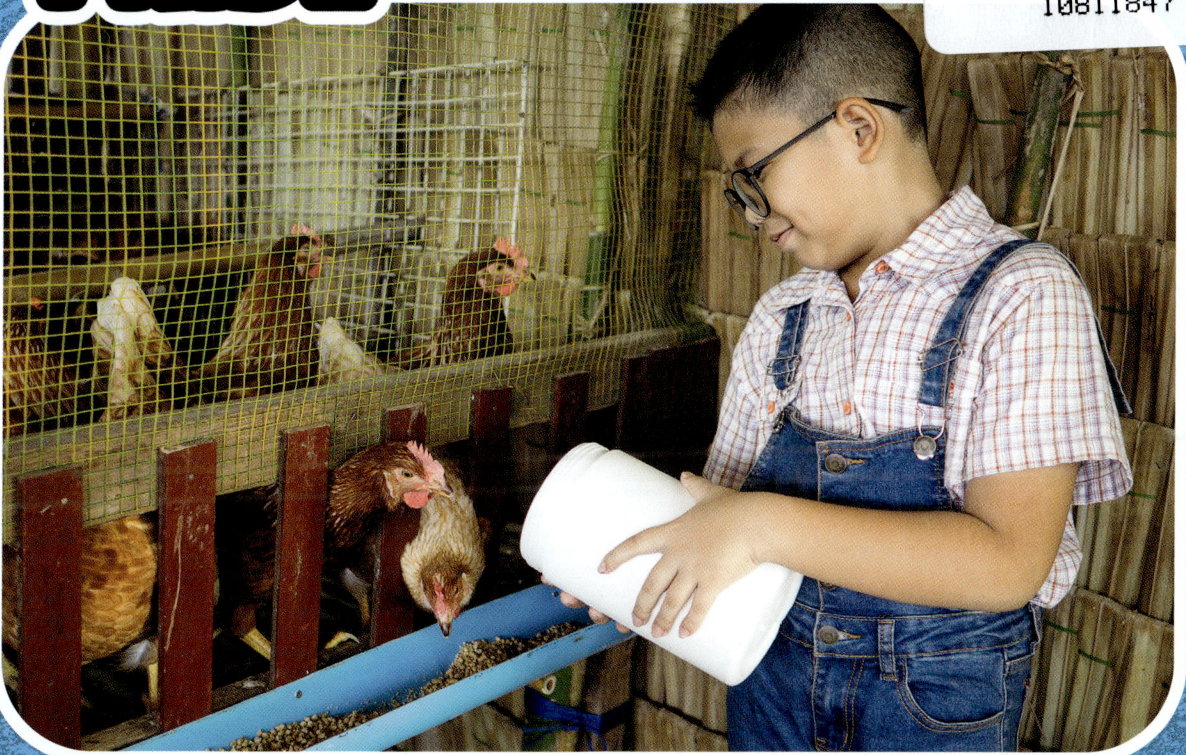

Andrew Lasda

PowerKiDS press

Published in 2025 by The Rosen Publishing Group, Inc.
2544 Clinton Street, Buffalo, NY 14224

Editor: Michele Suchomel-Casey
Book Design: Leslie Taylor

Photo Credits: Cover JoonKaltanida/Shutterstock.com; (series background) P.siripak/Shutterstock.com; (series disability pride colors) rudall30/Shutterstock.com; p. 5 r.classen/Shutterstock.com, (inset flag) Maxim Studio/Shutterstock.com; p. 7 a katz/ Shutterstock.com, (inset) Unknown Author/File:Bush signs in ADA of 1990.jpg_commons.wikimedia.org; p. 9 fotografixx/ iStockphoto.com, (inset) Zipster969, pawsitivityservicedogs.com/File:Thetheringautism.jpg_commons.wikimedia.org; p. 11 (upper) gillmar/Shutterstock.com, (lower) Roman Zaiets/Shutterstock.com; p. 13 SeventyFour/iStockphoto.com; p. 15 Jacob Lund/Shutterstock.com; p. 17 Halfpoint/Shutterstock.com; p. 19 Deciccio, Kate, Artist, Sponsor Amplifier, and Publisher Amplifier. We the Future - Are Building Disability Justice. , 2020. [Seattle: Amplifier] Photograph. https://www.loc.gov/item/2021635606/; p. 21 HTWE/Shutterstock.com.

Cataloging-in-Publication Data

Names: Lasda, Andrew.
Title: Independence matters / Andrew Lasda.
Description: Buffalo, NY : PowerKids Press, 2025. | Series: Disability pride | Includes glossary and index.
Identifiers: ISBN 9781499446807 (pbk.) | ISBN 9781499446814 (library bound) | ISBN 9781499446821 (ebook)
Subjects: LCSH: People with disabilities–Juvenile literature. | People with disabilities–Social conditions–Juvenile literature. | Disabilities–Juvenile literature.
Classification: LCC HV1568.L373 2025 | DDC 362.4–dc23

Manufactured in the United States of America

Some of the images in this book illustrate individuals who are models. The depictions do not imply actual situations or events.

CPSIA Compliance Information: Batch #CSPK25. For Further Information contact Rosen Publishing at 1-800-237-9932.

Contents

About Disabilities

Disabilities affect about 42.5 million Americans, and these disabilities vary in how they appear. Some disabilities affect people physically, such as lasting issues with an arm or leg, severe joint stiffness, or **damage** to the spine or an organ like the lungs.

Other disabilities affect the brain and aren't something other people can see easily. These disabilities come out in the person's behavior or ability to learn. They include difficulties with reading or numbers, or having trouble going places and doing everyday things.

Disabilities can be something people are born with, or they can happen after an accident or illness. Because of these disabilities, people may struggle with **independence**.

The disability pride flag was created to show acceptance and respect for people who have disabilities. Each color is for a different type of disability.

- The gray background is in honor of those who've died.
- Green is for disabilities that have to do with the senses.
- Blue is for those that have to with the mind and emotions.
- White stands for unseen disabilities, as well as those that haven't been diagnosed, or found out.
- Gold is for neurodiversity.
- Red is for other disabilities of the body.

Anyone can have a disability, and you can't always tell who has one. About 13 percent of Americans, or just over one in ten, has a disability.

The ADA

The U.S. Congress signed the Americans with Disabilities Act (ADA) into law in 1990. It provides many legal protections, defines reasonable **accommodations**, and outlaws **discrimination** against those with disabilities. Since the law was passed, it has been **amended** to clear up the definition of what a disability is as well as to define the goal of the law to make it broad and **inclusive**.

While the ADA has helped improve the independence of people with disabilities by putting access to public buildings and transportation into law and outlawing discrimination for having a disability, many disability rights groups feel there is still work to be done.

Learn More

The ADA is a lengthy law that took decades to be passed by Congress. President George H. W. Bush signed the ADA into law on July 26, 1990. Amendments were made in 2008 and 2019.

At right, President Bush signs the ADA into law on the White House South Lawn in 1990. Below, the disabled community protests for more rights in New York City.

Accommodations

Independence is being able to live life without help from other people. Disability independence is having the necessary accommodations to enjoy and go about everyday life. Many accommodations for disabilities in the United States came about because of the ADA.

Accommodations can take many different forms. Making sure there are ramps for people in wheelchairs to enter a building and elevators to take them to other floors are examples of physical accommodations. Other accommodations might include allowing a guide dog into an office or letting people have **flexible** work hours so they can go to medical appointments.

Guide dogs help people get around and have more independence. Don't pet guide dogs without the owner's permission—they're working!

In the Past

Before the ADA, there were no federal protections for people with disabilities. Many of the things we take for granted today did not exist. Closed captioning, the words at the bottom of the screen of TV shows, did not exist before the ADA. This meant that people who were deaf or hard of hearing couldn't enjoy TV shows or receive news broadcasts.

Before the ADA, public transportation, such as buses, was largely **inaccessible** if someone was in a wheelchair. Public buildings often did not have ramps or **automatic** doors, meaning that a wheelchair could not come in. Not having these accommodations created discrimination against people with disabilities.

Learn More

The ADA doesn't cover building standards for nonpublic housing, meaning that most houses are not up to code for people with mobility, or movement, disabilities.

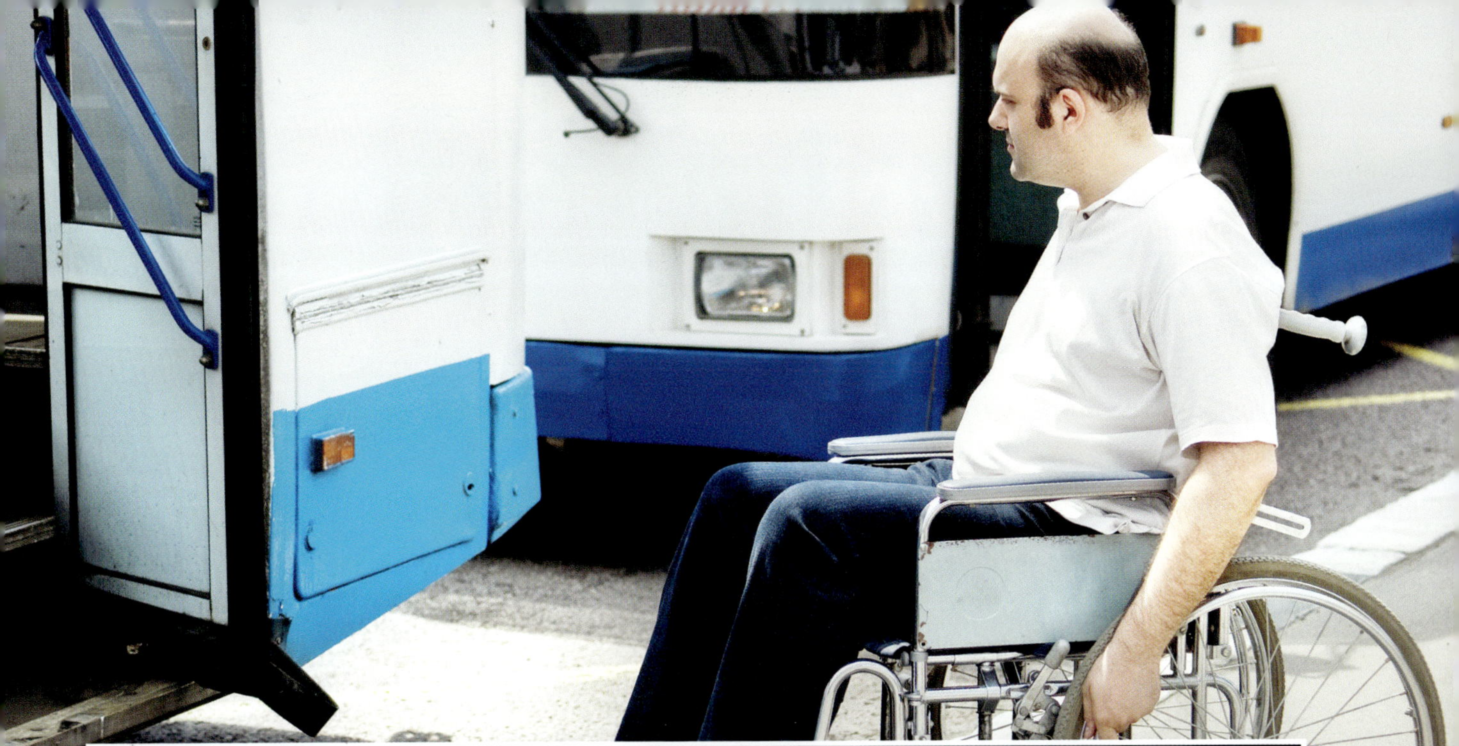

Thanks to the ADA, improved designs have helped people who use wheelchairs to access public buildings and transportation.

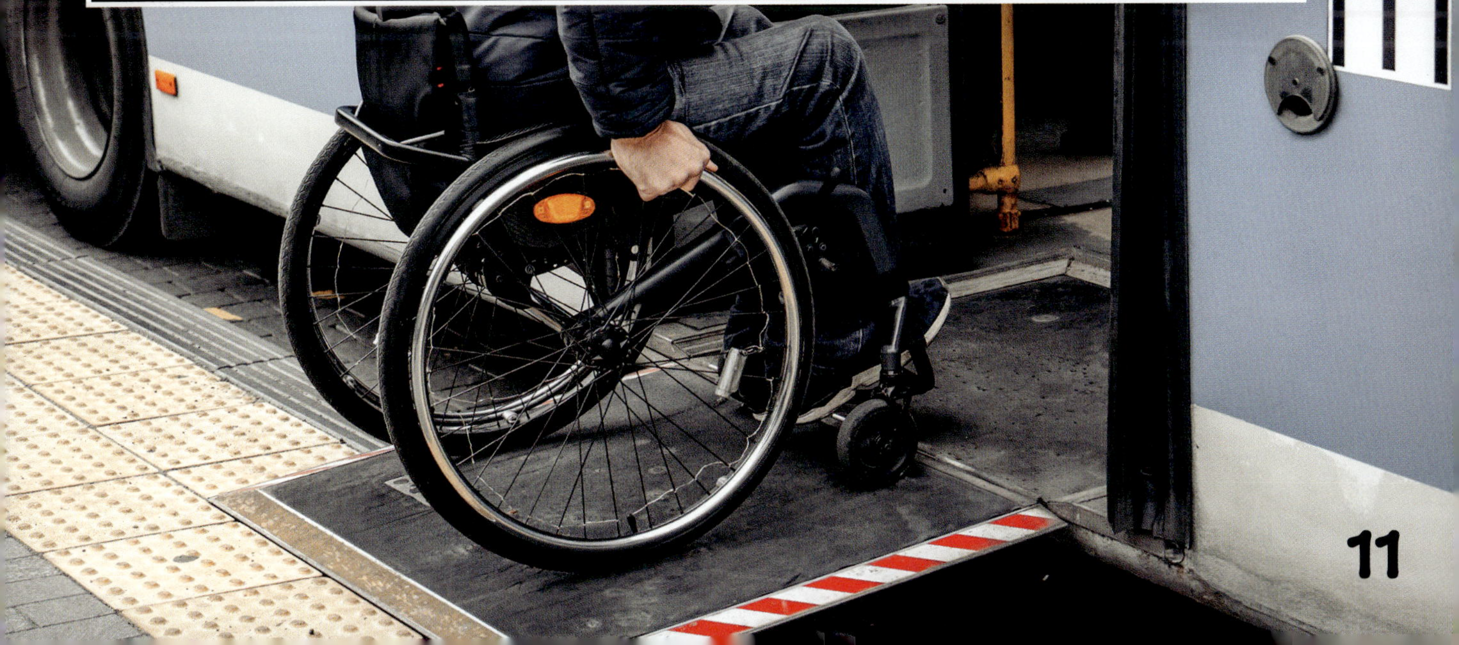

Discrimination Hurts Independence

Discrimination means treating someone worse or differently than another person because they have a certain **attribute**. There are many different ways people with disabilities have been discriminated against in the past that are now illegal. Using an earlier example, buildings without ramps discriminate against people who use wheelchairs.

Sometimes discrimination may be an accident, something that people without a disability might not think about. Other times it can be on purpose, like not hiring someone for a job they are able to do, because of their disability. Both kinds of disability discrimination are harmful and illegal and prevent people from being independent.

Many places remain inaccessible to people with mobility issues.

Learn More

About 30 percent of people with disabilities were found to have had difficulties voting in the 2012 election, versus 8.4 percent of people without disabilities.

Limits to Independence

Being independent means having your own money and your own home and being able to take care of yourself. People with disabilities deserve to have the same opportunities, or chances, as anyone else. Ensuring access to jobs for people with disabilities helps make sure they can have their own money and place to live.

However, some disabilities can limit people to jobs that don't pay well or can keep people from having jobs at all. Other disabilities keep people from being able to do things around the house, like cook, do laundry, or wash themselves.

Learn More

About 9 million U.S. workers have a disability, and on average they earn 13 percent less than non-disabled workers doing the same job.

People with disabilities are capable of doing many of the things non-disabled can do, including earning their own income at a full-time job.

Disability Benefits

To assist people with disabilities in being independent, there are government programs that help provide the basics. Social Security Disability Insurance (SSDI) is a program that provides monthly income and sometimes medical help through **Medicare**. Families that have someone with a disability can also apply for housing assistance that can help with rent or go toward changing a home to make it more accessible and safer for the person with the disability.

However, many people feel that the programs aren't helpful enough to people with disabilities. SSDI payments are often not enough to maintain a basic lifestyle and can't pay for larger expenses such as having an in-home aide or nurse.

Many older people require additional help in their own homes.

Learn More

The average monthly SSDI payment in 2019 was $1,234, or $14,808 annually. This was barely enough to take care of basic needs.

Advocacy Groups and Goals

While disability **advocates** have had success in getting laws passed that help people with disabilities, groups like the American Association of People with Disabilities (AAPD) are still fighting for many goals. These goals include encouraging people with disabilities to advocate for themselves, continuing improvements in the law for housing and transportation, and providing affordable health care and the right of individuals to make decisions about their own care.

The AAPD creates a way for people with disabilities to become organized and fight for their rights. By doing this, it allows people with disabilities to put pressure on lawmakers to act in their interests.

Disability advocates like Lydia X.Z. Brown help improve the visibility of people with disabilities and their legal issues.

The Importance of Independence

People with disabilities deserve the same dignity and respect as anyone else. By supporting independence for everyone, we are making a fairer and better society. While there have been major successes in passing laws, such as the ADA, there is still a lot of work to be done in stopping disability discrimination and providing everyone with the basics for living.

By becoming aware of the challenges to independence that people with disabilities face, you can help! Become an advocate! By supporting the cause of disability independence, you help yourself and your neighbors. Chances are, you know someone who has a disability, even if you can't see it.

Being an advocate is a great way to help someone with a disability.

Glossary

accommodation: A change or adjustment to help someone.

advocate: A person who argues for or supports a cause or policy.

amend: To make small changes to a document or bill.

attribute: A characteristic or quality.

automatic: Having technology that permits operation without help from a person.

damage: Loss or harm to a person or property.

discrimination: Unfair treatment based on factors such as a person's race, age, religion, or gender.

flexible: Capable of being changed with little notice.

inaccessible: Hard or impossible to reach or access.

inclusive: Including as many people as possible.

independence: Freedom from outside control or support.

Medicare: A U.S. health insurance program for people 65 or older and for people with disabilities.

For More Information

BOOKS

Finke, Beth. *What Is the Americans with Disabilities Act?* Ann Arbor, MI: Cherry Lake Press, 2023.

Pimentel, Annette Bay. *All the Way to the Top: How One Girl's Fight for Americans with Disabilities Changed Everything*. Naperville IL: Sourcebooks Explore, 2020.

Rea, Amy C. *Living with Learning Disabilities*. San Diego, CA: ReferencePoint Press, 2019.

WEBSITES

American Association of People with Disabilities
www.aapd.com
This nonprofit organization advocates and lobbies for the civil rights of people with disabilities.

Individuals with Disabilities Education Act
sites.ed.gov/idea
The U.S. Department of Education's Individuals with Disabilities Education Act (IDEA) website contains articles about the laws regarding disabilities, locating local resources, and providing data on various categories of children with disabilities.

UNICEF
www.unicef.org/disabilities
UNICEF provides information on children with disabilities and the discrimination they face.

Index